# BUGS AND SLUGS

Judy Tatchell

Illustrated by Justine Torode

Designed by Ruth Russell and Jane Rigby

Digital imaging by Keith Furnival

# Bees and wasps

Can you find a bee on this page? It's collecting a sweet liquid called nectar from a flower.

Wasps love sweet things. They are a nuisance if they come after your food.

Wasp

If a wasp or bee is scared, it might sting, so don't try to hit it.

This is a bumble bee. It is looking for nectar.

Is that a bee or a wasp on the peach? Lift the flap to see.

# Spiders

Spiders eat flies and other insects. They make sticky webs to catch them.

A spider makes a new web each morning.

Spiders have oily feet. These stop them from getting stuck in their webs.

This fly has just flown into the web.

# Worms

Worms break up soil as they burrow. This helps plants push their roots into the soil.

It isn't easy to tell which end of a worm is the front!

A worm moves by stretching out the front of its body.

Front of worm

Back of worm

Then it pulls the back part forward.

# Butterflies

Butterflies lay eggs on leaves. Out of each egg comes a tiny caterpillar.

The tiny caterpillar eats the leaves.

It makes a case around itself. Inside, it turns into a butterfly.

Case

# Ladybugs and aphids

Ladybugs are easy to see. You can count their spots.

Ladybugs like to eat aphids. Can you see a ladybug having a snack?

If the ladybug eats all the aphids...

Aphids suck a liquid, called sap, from buds. The buds dry up. A dry bud won't open into a flower.

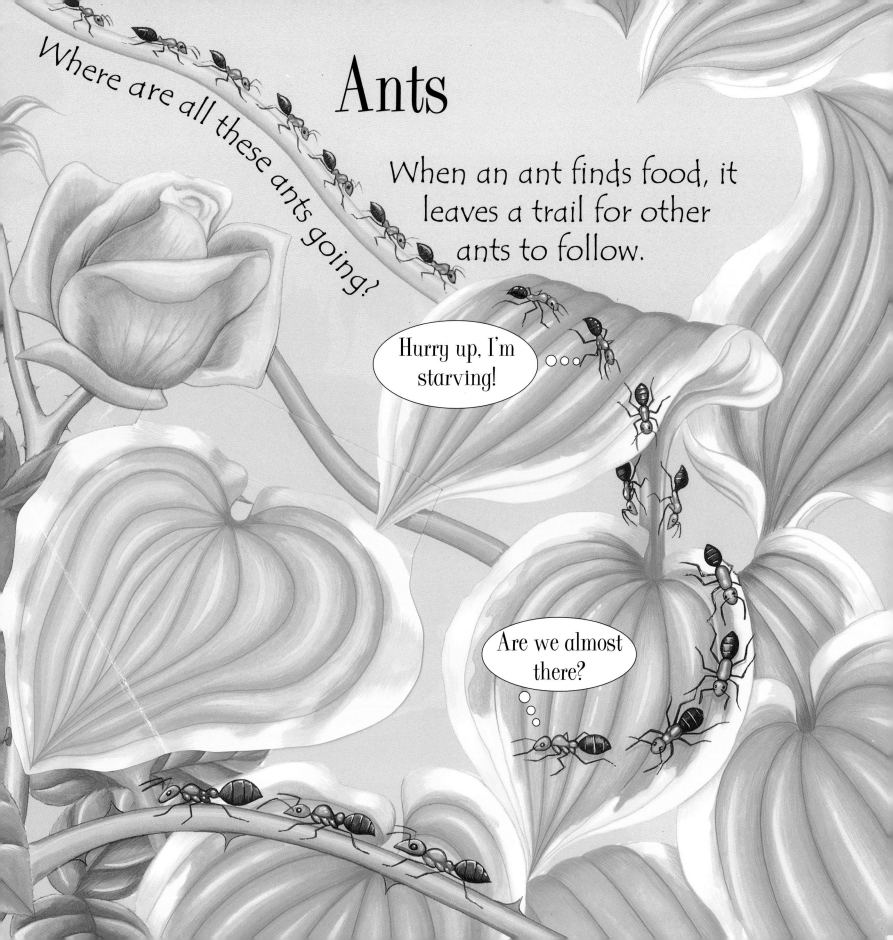

# Slugs and snails

Slugs and snails like damp, cool places.

What's eating this lettuce?

Munch Munch

Snails can't see well, but they are good at smelling and feeling.

I'm safe in here!

Some birds eat snails. They have to break the shell.

Who's at the end of this shiny trail?

If snails and slugs dry out, they can't make slime.

A snail's shell helps stop it from drying out in the sun.

# Beetles

Beetles like to live among leaves and sticks. They eat tiny insects.

Wing case

A beetle has two hard, shiny wing cases over its wings. These keep its wings safe.

Wing case

When a beetle flies, it holds its wing cases out of the way.

# Centipedes and millipedes

Centipede

A centipede is very wriggly. It eats smaller creatures. It has to run quickly to catch its food.

Millipede

A millipede eats plants. It has more legs than a centipede but it can't run as quickly!

Whose tail is this?

This book has shown you just some of the
tiny creatures that you can find living in
your yard. Why not explore for yourself
to see how many more you can discover?

Buzzzzzzzzzzz

Edited by Sarah Khan

This new, enlarged edition first published in 2004 by Usborne Publishing Ltd, Usborne House,
83-85 Saffron Hill, London EC1N 8RT, England.
www.usborne.com
Copyright © Usborne Publishing Ltd, 2004, 1999. First published in America 2004. AE

Printed in China.

zzz